T0039194

ANGEL

PRACTITIONER HANDBOOK

A Foundation Guide

Revised Edition

MARIA G. MAAS

BALBOA.PRESS

A DIVISION OF HAY HOUSE

Balboa Press books may be ordered through booksellers or by contacting:

Balboa Press
A Division of Hay House
1663 Liberty Drive
Bloomington, IN 47403
www.balboapress.com
844-682-1282

Print information available on the last page.

ISBN: 978-1-5043-4684-9 (sc)
ISBN: 978-1-5043-4685-6 (e)

Library of Congress Control Number: 2015920687

Balboa Press rev. date: 02/09/2024

ABOUT THIS BOOK

Angel Practitioner Handbook: A Foundation Guide is a comprehensive resource that provides the necessary knowledge and techniques for anyone who wants to work with angels.

Learn how to:

- Enhance your spiritual connection with the angelic realm to receive Divine guidance, healing, and protection.
- Understand and work with the law of vibration (LOV)
- Communicate with your guardian angel.
- Improve your intuition and develop your psychic abilities as you discover and expand your unique gifts.
- Identify angel crystals and decode angel numbers.
- Perform angel readings for yourself and others.
- Build confidence in your skills as an angel practitioner and more!

Author and angel specialist Maria G. Maas also designed this guide as a companion manual to the *Certified Angel Practitioner™ Course*. Ms. Maas is the founding president of the *International Association of Angel Practitioners (IAAP)* and AngelPractitioners.com. She hosted *Angelic Realms Radio* and now hosts *The Angelic View Show*. She is also the author and creator of *The Angelic View Oracle Cards with Guidebook & Journal*.

For more information on becoming a *Certified Angel Practitioner™* via the *IAAP*, email the author, Maria G. Maas, at Maria@MariaGMaas.com or visit https://www. AngelPractitioners.com/Courses

DEDICATION

For Nanny & Louis, who'll forever live in my heart and are always with me in spirit.

Acknowledgements

Words cannot express my thanks and appreciation for my darling husband, Arthur, whom I know was heaven-sent to me. He has lovingly and unselfishly supported and encouraged me for the past thirty-one years (and counting) in all I have wanted to accomplish and the things I still intend to do. He is the voice of reason when I get crazy, my sense of calm when I get anxious, and motivator when I get discouraged. He is a wonderful life partner with a gift for listening and understanding. He is highly intuitive and sometimes even knows me better than I know myself.

I am grateful to my husband, Arthur, for all the encouragement he gives to me and for being so patient with me throughout the writing and revisions of this book, the creation of the *Certified Angel Practitioner Course* (both the original and 2nd edition), and the design of *The Angelic View Oracle Cards* deck. I appreciate the endless hours he has spent brainstorming with me, helping me to organize my thoughts and ideas, and taking over chores for me so that I could have more time to devote to these projects.

I also want to thank my friend and colleague, Dax Carlisle, for teaching me how to host and manage a live

Internet radio show. I also appreciate his support in joining me as a cofounder of the *International Association of Angel Practitioners (IAAP)*.

I am especially thankful to God for the many gifts I have received and His continued blessings for my loved ones and me. I greatly appreciate my angels and spirit guides for prompting me to take on this work and inspiring me to complete it.

CONTENTS

PREFACE

My name is Maria G. Maas, and as the president and cofounder of *The International Association of Angel Practitioners (IAAP)*, I am delighted to present an updated edition of the "Angel Practitioner Handbook: A Foundation Guide." As an angel-intuitive medium, spiritual teacher, and the creator and instructor of the *Certified Angel Practitioner™ (CAP™) Course*, my life has been intertwined with threads of Divine inspiration and guidance.

Initially published in April 2016, this handbook has been revised and revitalized. The text flows more freely, creating an easy read. I have added new content, enhancing the depth and breadth of this spiritual guide with additional practical exercises to foster the reader's learning experience. I've also shared some stories of my personal experiences with angelic intervention and messages from the spirit world.

May this handbook lead you to a deeper understanding of the Divine powers surrounding us and empower you to embark on a sacred spiritual journey as you connect with angels of love, light, strength, protection, healing, abundance, and wisdom.

Angel blessings,
~ Maria

Introduction

The *Angel Practitioner Handbook: A Foundation Guide* was my inspiration for quite some time. I wrote this book with two purposes in mind. The first is a companion handbook to The *Certified Angel Practitioner*^{TM} *Course.* The second serves as a guide to anyone interested in learning how to connect with angels for everyday guidance.

My angels have helped me every step of the way. My first experience was receiving their loving assistance and healing during a time of intense grief in my life that followed with the angels blending their wisdom and guidance into my tarot readings. The angels continue to keep the passion alive within me to learn more about them, how to work with them, and to assist others who feel the calling to work with the angels as *lightworkers* – those predestined to be born into one or more lifetimes on Earth to help humanity, the animal kingdom, and the environment.

I created the *Certified Angel Practitioner Course,* also called *CAP*^{TM} *Course,* because I saw a need for an affordable and comprehensive course for those seeking to learn how to work with the angels. In 2015, many regular listeners to my live call-in show, *Angelic Realms Radio,* which aired weekly at the time, had also expressed an interest in my course and book.

This book contains notes that are relevant to the *CAP Course*. It is also for anyone who would like to learn how to work with angels for personal guidance. Inside this book, you will find five exercises that I have created to help you to put into practice the information and techniques presented here. I have also included prayers and guided meditations that I wrote specifically for the material and methods that I introduce in this book. As an added resource, I have included some handy charts that I put together so that you can refer to them at-a-glance for a quick reference.

Please understand that no course or book will make you a *lightworker*. You cannot train someone to be a *lightworker*. Becoming a *lightworker* is a calling, and the desire is innate. What my course and book will provide you with is some background knowledge about the angelic realms and the techniques that will enable you, as a lightworker, to work more effectively with the angels.

This book and the course will equip the individual with the knowledge and tools necessary to be an angel practitioner; it is up to the individual to continue building upon the knowledge shared here and hone their skills. Anything that one seeks to do well takes desire, passion, practice, patience, determination, discernment, a commitment to expertise, self-confidence, faith in God, and a loving and grateful heart.

Exercise #1

Answer the following question honestly from your heart center:

Why do you want to be an angel practitioner?

<u>Your Notes</u>:

ANGELOLGY FAQS

What is angelology? *Angelology* is the study of angels.

What are angels? The term "angel" comes from the Greek word "angelos," which translates to "messengers." The term "angel" ends in "el," which comes from the Hebrew term "El," which translates to "of God" and has been used generically as one of the names for God. Some other names for God are "Elohim," "El Shaddai," and "Yahweh," to name a few. The term "angel" means "messenger of God." Angels are extensions of God's pure love and light. Angels transcend many different faiths of some of the world's major religions like Christianity, Judaism, Islam, and others.

Why did God create angels? God created the angels to serve Him.

When did God create angels? According to the *Bible*, some say that it was on the first day of creation when God said, "Let there be light." Others believe that it is referenced in the *Bible* to have been on the second day of creation. Is this accurate? How can anyone say for sure? I have to ask you, though, "Is it important for us to know exactly when God created the angels?" It's a matter of faith. What matters is that they exist, and their purpose is to serve God. In doing so, God has created certain angels to assist humanity. They can help those who allow them into their lives in many ways, from the small day-to-day things like finding a good parking space to the grander things like fulfilling one's Divine life purpose.

Are there a limited number of angels? No. I believe that God creates angels as needed. For example, when we call upon Archangel Raphael, whose name means "Healing of God" or "God Heals," we are sending out a prayer asking God to bring healing. Archangel Raphael is in charge of millions of healing angels. If it is God's will to answer our prayer, Archangel Raphael can call as many healing angels to action as needed on our behalf. There is never a shortage of angels.

What are the Nine Choirs of Angels? The nine choirs of angels are the hierarchy that angels exist in the order of their service to God. There are three spheres or levels.

The First Sphere

The first sphere of angels, in general, is most concerned with the glory of God. The first sphere is the closest to God, and the *seraphim*, the *cherubim*, and the *thrones* are in this sphere. The *seraphim* are the highest-ranking angels. The *seraphim's* primary existence is to praise God and serve as His agents of purification. Their songs of praise to Him ring aloud with constant echoes that never cease. The light is the brightest; the vibration here is the highest. The love is perpetual.

The initial responsibility of the *cherubim* was protecting the *Garden of Eden*, as referenced in the book of *Genesis*. The *cherubim*, whose name translates to "fullness of wisdom," contemplate and communicate God's Divine plan for His creation. In some traditions, *cherubim* also pray to God on man's behalf, asking Him to forgive and protect the righteous.

The *thrones* are among the angels with the highest knowledge of the works of God and regarded worthy of direct fellowship with Jesus. As beings of the first sphere, these angels can convey the entire essence of God's word, passing the messages to the lower classes of angels who share them with people.

The Second Sphere

In the second sphere reside the *dominions*, the *virtues*, and the *powers*. The angels in this sphere maintain the laws of the universe and cosmic order. The *dominions* (also known as *dominations*) oversee the lower angelic hierarchy. The *virtues* inspire goodwill and supervise the movement of heavenly bodies like the sun, stars, and planets. The powers preside over *karmic* law and are the keepers of the *akashic* records, which hold all the history of the created universe and every soul that has ever existed.

The Third Sphere

The third sphere is closest to Earth and humanity. In this sphere reside the principalities, the archangels, and the angels. The principalities are angels that guide and protect nations, cities, and organizations like churches. The archangels are the supervisors of the angelic kingdom and God's messengers and helpers for humanity. Then there are angels like the angels of abundance, faith, love, peace, etc., and guardian angels that have been assigned to you personally when your soul came into existence and remained with you throughout all your incarnations. The guiding angels work with you and change as you evolve spiritually. As angel practitioners, we work primarily with the angels of the third sphere.

Do angels have free will? Yes. It is the will of most angels to serve God. There are, however, fallen angels who have strayed from God. These fallen angels are not the angels that we want to influence us in any way. It is essential to protect yourself and your clients from negative energies <u>before</u> opening up to the forces in the spirit realm. We will explore some grounding and protection techniques later in this book.

What do angels look like - do they have wings? Ancient mystics, prophets, and channelers perceived angelic auras as wings. Angels are pure spirit energy that God has granted the ability to transform into any form they choose. You may encounter an angel and not even know it. They can appear as another flesh and blood human being who can arrive momentarily on the scene to keep someone out of harm's way if it is God's will. Very often, angels appear as balls of white or colored light. These balls of light can vary in size. Sometimes they can appear as tiny sparkles of white or colored lights. Angels can also show themselves as fearsome creatures when necessary to defend God's will and the Heavenly realms.

How long ago were the angels named? The oldest evidence is in the Aramaic texts amongst the *Dead Sea Scrolls*, which contained lists of angel names of the holy angels and the fallen ones. These texts are fragments of the first book of Enoch, the great-grandfather of Noah, and date back as far as somewhere around 300 B.C.

Why call upon angels when you can call upon God directly? Some people believe that because there are fallen angels, humans may be subject to trickery and should call upon God directly. However, most will agree that there are well-known angels that are trustworthy. I encourage you to call upon these angels primarily. There is nothing to fear. The angels discussed in this book are "of God" and extensions of His pure love and light.

During meditation with my guardian angel and Archangel Gabriel, I learned that working with them and other angels like them is just as safe and effective as calling upon God directly. These are angels who are a part of God and how God can be everywhere and help everyone simultaneously. As angels of the third sphere, these angels are close enough to our earthly realm for us to be able to communicate with them. It is easier for us to comprehend their messages than we can perceive God's direction because they are vibrating at a frequency closer to our own. These angels are our spiritual connection between Heaven and Earth.

Why should you invite angels into your life? The angels can assist you in your communication with God and help you understand and accept God's will. Inviting angels into your life will help build a stronger connection between yourself and God.

Angels are always ready to help you at any given moment. There is nothing too big or small when calling upon your angels for assistance. There is no need to feel guilty about calling upon them for something minor because there are others who may need them for something more significant. They can help us all simultaneously. Angels are nonjudgmental and only wish to serve God's will and help us with whatever we want or need for our highest good. When you invite the angels into your life, you will gain a greater sense of well-being and know that you are never really alone.

Vibrational Energy and How It Affects Our Ability To Communicate With Our Angels

What is vibrational energy?

The *Universal/Cosmic Law of Vibration (LOV)* is the foundation of the more well-known *Universal/Cosmic Law of Attraction (LOA).* According to the LOA, "like attracts like," meaning that whatever energy you send out attracts the same kind of energy back to you. The LOV states, "All that exists, seen or unseen, has vibrational energy." Everything has vibrational energy, whether living, spirit, or inanimate. The rate at which the energy vibrates varies. Thoughts, feelings, and seemingly empty or blank spaces have a vibrational rate.

How does vibrational energy affect you?

Vibrational energy can be low or high. Lower vibrational energy is negative, and higher vibrational energy is typically more positive. The angels vibrate at a very high rate of energy.

To attract the angels and enhance angelic communication, raise your vibrational energy. Increasing your vibrational energy enhances one's ability to receive messages from the angels, and at the same time, it makes it easier for the angels to assist.

Angels are pure ethereal beings and are attracted to and sensed best by those who can raise their vibrations high enough to achieve the state of consciousness necessary for angelic communication. Your vibrational rate can either boost or hinder the ability of the angels to work with you. It does not mean that if your vibrational energy falls low, the angels will not be able to help you; it's just easier for them to assist you the higher your vibrational energy.

How can you raise your vibrational energy?

The list below provides some ways that you can boost your vibrational energy. They are not listed in any particular order of preference or effectiveness, nor are the suggestions listed conclusive. The tips that follow are just some ideas to get you started.

Tips for Raising Your Vibrational Energy:

- Ask the angels to help you raise your vibrational energy
- De-clutter your space
- Clean your space
- Smudge with sage
- Splash holy water
- Let in the fresh air

- Spend time outdoors
- Spray your area with essential oil sprays like cypress or rose.
- Adjust lighting
- Use color
- Play music
- Sing
- Dance
- Join a drumming circle
- Take a walk
- Play with your children or pets
- Read encouraging books and articles
- Eat healthy foods
- Draw, paint, or spend time doing some other creative and enjoyable activity
- Listen to an upbeat radio show or podcast
- Watch an inspirational movie or TV show
- Listen to a motivational sermon
- Look at adorable photos of babies or animals
- Keep a gratitude journal
- Write a thank you letter to your guardian angel
- Say a prayer to God, Jesus, Mother Mary, a beloved saint, or any benevolent higher power you trust
- Keep crystals like celestite, selenite, and angelite nearby
- Meditate
- Avoid negative people and media as much as possible.

Creating Sacred Space

Everything in the physical world consists of energy vibrating at different rates; you want to create the best conditions possible to enhance angelic communication. It will be beneficial to set aside a special place that you keep just for connecting with your angels. This space does not even have to be an entire room. It can be a small space within an area where you can sit quietly and not be interrupted. It doesn't even have to be indoors. A comfortable outdoor space can be ideal.

Of course, there will be times when you will not have access to your own sacred space; for instance, when you are sitting with a client, depending on where the meeting is taking place, there can be times when you might not have this luxury. Even if you are doing readings in a public setting, it doesn't mean you won't be able to access angelic guidance. With practice, you will be able to raise your vibrations enough to do so when and wherever necessary.

Setting Up an Angel Altar

Once you have your location selected for your sacred space, it will be helpful to define that space with something concrete that will enable you to focus your thoughts and energy. A small table, shelf, desk, or tray will do. A tray is portable, so if you'd like to take advantage of being able to move your space outdoors on a nice day, this can be very handy.

You can keep items that will attract loving and harmonious energy on your altar. Some things to consider placing on your altar are:

- Crystals like selenite or angelite
- Angel figurines
- Candles (use caution with candles, especially if you have small children or pets – don't leave a burning candle unattended)
- Holy water
- Rosary beads
- Flowers
- Feathers
- Photographs of loved ones or pets
- Seashells

You can use just about anything that inspires you and helps you feel peaceful and joyful. I suggest including something representing each of the following elements - earth, air, fire, water, and spirit. Here's an example:

- Earth - flower
- Air - feather
- Fire - candle
- Water - holy water
- Spirit - angel figurine

How to Deal with Unwanted/Negative Vibrational Energy

Let's face it, we're only human, and at times, we all experience the effects of unwanted vibrational energy – some of us more so than others. The degree to which the negative energy affects us depends on many variables, and exposure to this negative vibrational energy may often be unavoidable.

You may find that your work environment is negative – possibly even toxic. Perhaps someone you live with is an extremely negative person. You could happen to be a worrywart. Maybe horror flicks entertain you. Does this mean that you should quit your job, move out of your home, or never watch a scary movie again? No. That wouldn't be very practical. Although depending on your circumstances, it could be vital to do so; however, in many cases, that wouldn't be necessary.

Just as I offered some tips earlier for raising vibrational energy to a more positive state, the list below provides some ways that you can cleanse/release negative vibrational energy. The list is not in any particular order of preference or effectiveness, nor are the suggestions listed conclusive. You will find that some of these suggestions overlap with the ideas mentioned previously for raising positive vibrational energy. Again, the following tips are just some ideas to get you started.

Suggestions for Cleansing Yourself of Unwanted /Negative Energy:

- Splash yourself or your space with holy water
- Smudge your space with sage

- Take a salt bath
- Say a prayer
- Avoid negative people or media
- Eliminate fatty and unnatural foods
- Reduce exposure to air and noise pollution
- Burn a white candle (I like using a Himalayan Sea salt candle holder)
- Spend some time outdoors
- Open the window and let in some fresh air and natural light
- De-clutter your space
- Clean your space
- Meditate with the angels
- Spray your space with a sage spray or other essential oil spray like frankincense
- Ask your angels, especially Archangel Michael, to cleanse and detoxify your space.

Grounding and Protecting Yourself

Before doing any psychic work or opening oneself up to the spiritual world, it is imperative to ground and protect yourself. Better still, it's a good idea to make this a daily habit, as we are all at risk of encountering negative energy that we can absorb. It is also beneficial to know how to protect yourself from psychic attacks when someone sends negative thoughts to you. This type of protection will also guard you against being overwhelmed by the energy of someone who might be a psychic vampire, i.e., a person who is very emotionally draining.

The act of grounding yourself means to connect to the earth and the here and now. When we become ungrounded, we may feel dizzy, unfocused, unbalanced, or spacey. We want to bring our awareness and focus back to the here and now to ground ourselves.

Here are some things we can do to ground ourselves:

- Stamp your feet on the floor
- Clap your hands
- Grasp or tap on the arms or seat of your chair
- Get some fresh air
- Hug a tree
- Kneel or squat and place the palms of your hands on the earth
- Visualize roots growing from your feet and extending down into the earth
- Hold and feel a particular piece of jewelry or a grounding crystal like red jasper, unakite, or hematite
- Take a drink of cool water
- Eat something natural that comes from the earth

We're all connected by spirit. We all have the potential to absorb vibrational energies, both positive and negative. When we protect ourselves spiritually and psychically, we shield ourselves from lower/negative entities and powers from the spirit realm. We also protect ourselves from absorbing negative vibrational energy on the physical earth plane. Just because someone doesn't do spiritual work or consider themself psychic doesn't mean they are any less capable of being vulnerable to the effects of negative energy.

<u>Here is an activity you can do to protect yourself from absorbing negative vibrational energy</u>:

1. Call upon Archangel Michael, your guardian angel, God the Father, Jesus, Mother Mary, or a trusted saint (Saint Therese, Saint Christopher, etc.). Ask this loving being to shield you from any negative energy you may encounter throughout your day.

   Note: Since I'm Catholic, these are my recommendations. If you're of a different faith, call upon the higher power you trust.

2. Envision yourself encased inside a sphere of bright blue light.
3. Thank the benevolent being for its protection.
4. You can boost the shielding power by wearing something blue or carrying a blue crystal.
5. You might also wear a hematite necklace or bracelet. The hematite color doesn't matter because it is gleaming and reflective, thus acting as a mirror that deflects the negative energy.

I suggest saying a prayer or meditating (example to follow). Prayer is a form of meditation. Even just a few minutes of prayer can be considered meditation. When we pray, we focus our thoughts on the desired outcome. The more deeply we pray, the higher the meditative state we can achieve. We can begin to visualize what we want in answer to our prayers. When we pray with conviction, we put our egos aside and give control to a higher power. The stronger our faith, the more likely we will receive the answer to our prayers. A strong faith allows the LOA to work for us instead of against us. Through the LOV, we speak the language of God and the angels.

The following is a prayer that I wrote to protect myself when I engage in any type of work that opens me up to the influence of the spirit world. Because I am Catholic, my prayer calls upon the higher power of my faith. This may not be suitable for you. Please take from it what serves your purpose and modify the rest as it fits with your beliefs.

Prayer to Raise Positive Energy and Repel Negative Energy

Holy Spirit, cleanse and protect me (visualize white light bathing you from head to toe). Mother Earth, ground me (visualize roots extending from your toes into the ground).

Mother Mary and Archangel Jophiel, please help raise my positive vibrations to attract more positive and higher energies and help me to radiate this positive energy (visualize golden sparkles of positive energy drawn to you like a magnet).

Jesus and Archangel Michael, please shield me from any lower energy coming near me. Repel it (visualize Archangel Michael raising his sword that shines like a mirror deflecting any negative energy away from you)! Neutralize it (as it bounces off his sword, it disintegrates)!

I ask this in the name of Jesus Christ, my Lord and Savior. Amen.

Now I am ready to go about my day and any business I may have, knowing that I am Divinely guided and protected.

Exercise #2

Now it is your turn to compose a prayer to prepare yourself to do a reading. This prayer should carry the intention to raise positive energy vibrations and shield both you and your client from negative energies.

<u>Your Notes</u>:

The Chakras and the Aura

For anyone who wants to do energy work, it is essential to understand the concept of chakras. The word *chakra* comes from the Sanskrit term for a *wheel*. The chakras are active energy centers associated with parts of your physical body and spiritual being.

The energy of the chakras spins in a circular motion, clockwise or counterclockwise. Masculine energies are said to turn clockwise, while feminine energies rotate counterclockwise. When the chakras become blocked, the spinning becomes off-balance. It can slow down, speed up, or reverse direction, causing us to feel "off." If not cleared or realigned, it can negatively affect one mentally, emotionally, physically, and spiritually.

There are many chakras, but for this book, I will focus on the seven main chakras that run along the spine and the eighth chakra, known as the soul-star chakra, which is the bridge between the earthly self and the Higher Self or Holy Spirit. I will discuss the colors that correspond to the chakras and the archangels associated with each of these chakras.

Here is a list of the seven main chakra colors and their meanings, as well as the soul star chakra and its color and meaning, that may be relevant for an angel practitioner:

1. **Root chakra** (color: red) - Associated with the sense of security and stability, physical vitality, and connection to the earth.
2. **Sacral chakra** (color: orange) - Associated with creativity, sexuality, and emotional well-being.
3. **Solar plexus chakra** (color: yellow) - Associated with personal power, self-esteem, and mental clarity.
4. **Heart chakra** (color: green or pink) - Associated with love, compassion, and connection to the Divine.
5. **Throat chakra** (color: blue) - Associated with communication, self-expression, and the ability to speak one's truth.
6. **Third eye chakra** (color: indigo) - Associated with intuition, wisdom, and the ability to see beyond the physical realm.
7. **Crown chakra** (color: violet or white) - Associated with spiritual connection, enlightenment, and the ability to connect with the Divine.
8. **Soul star chakra** (color: silver or gold) - Associated with the connection to the Divine, inspiration, and guidance from the higher self and spirit guides.

As an angel practitioner, understanding the meanings and associations of the chakra colors can help you to identify imbalances or blockages in the energy system of the person you are working with, and to facilitate healing and balance in the chakras. It can also help you to connect with the person's higher self and spirit guides, and to understand the messages they may be receiving from these sources.

The vital thing to understand about the chakras is that these energies are a part of our aura (see Figure 1). The human aura is an energy field that surrounds our physical bodies. That living part of us is the etheric body that allows us to sense other etheric beings who don't have a physical body. These etheric beings can be angels or even our departed loved ones. When we want to communicate with spiritual beings, we need to be able to expand our auras.

Angels are naturally attracted to high vibrational energy. When we expand our auras, it makes it easier for Spirit to communicate with us by blending with our aura. The higher we can raise our vibrational energy, the higher the realm of spiritual connections we can make. Because angels are extremely high vibrational spiritual beings, we need to push our auras out far enough to connect with them. When our vibrational energy is high, our aura can reach out far enough to communicate with the angels.

Here is a step-by-step guide for the angel practitioner to use to expand their aura for better communication with the angels and the spirit world:

1. Begin by setting an intention for the expansion of your aura, such as seeking a deeper connection with the angels and spirit guides.
2. Create a peaceful and relaxed atmosphere, either in person or remotely.
3. Sit or stand comfortably, and take a few deep breaths, focusing on your breath and allowing yourself to relax.

4. Invoke the angels of guidance and protection to assist in the process and ask them to help you to expand your aura and be open to their presence and guidance.

5. Place your hands on your heart chakra, and visualize a bright, white light entering and clearing your energy system.

6. Visualize your aura expanding outward from your body in all directions, like a glowing sphere.

7. Imagine your aura filling the room or space around you and visualize it connecting with the energy of the angels and spirit guides.

8. Focus on the sensation of your aura expanding and the energy of the angels and spirit guides flowing into and around you.

9. Spend a few minutes in this meditative state, focusing on the expansion of your aura and the connection with the angels and spirit guides.

10. End the practice by thanking the angels and spirit guides for their assistance and support, and by sealing the energy with a closing prayer or intention.

This is just one example of how an angel practitioner can use visualization and intention to expand their aura and connect with the angels and spirit guides. It is important to always follow your intuition and allow the guidance of the angels and spirit guides to lead the way in the process. It may also be helpful to incorporate other techniques, such as using crystals or essential oils, or practicing other forms of meditation or energy work.

Figure 1: The Chakras and the Aura

Accessing Divine Wisdom
And Angelic Guidance

After we have prepared ourselves to open to Spirit by shielding ourselves from negative energy and raising our positive vibrations, we now must quiet the ego. The ego is the part of our consciousness that interferes with angelic guidance. When the ego speaks, mental chatter goes on in our thinking, logical minds. It is the constant flow of thoughts that come and go. So, how do we stop this interference?

Here, the object is to get our minds into an "alpha state." We want to be in a semi-hypnotic state and not think of anything. We need to blank our minds as much as possible without falling asleep. While our angels communicate with us during our sleep, this will not be helpful when you are doing a reading for someone. We must relax our minds sufficiently to be receptive to guidance from our angels and alert enough to share the information we receive with our sitter/client.

Here are some ways to achieve this receptive state:

Guided meditation – Guided meditation is a highly effective means of preparing oneself to be open to receiving angelic guidance. You can find these meditations in books, on the Internet, or you can write your own.

It is helpful to meditate before beginning any reading scheduled for the day. Start with shorter meditations and increase the time as you progress. While daily meditation is ideal, some will not commit to this practice. If you commit to this practice, do not do your meditation while your client is present unless you want your client to take part in a short meditation with you. I once went for a reading, and the reader sat and meditated while I waited for my reading. I remember feeling annoyed having to sit in another room waiting for her to finish a 20-minute meditation.

Spend time outdoors – Spending time out in nature is ideal for opening to messages from the angels. There are many ways for them to send you messages while you're outdoors (more about signs from our angels later in this book). Sitting outside in a comfortable chair, where it is quiet and the sounds of nature can calm you, can be remarkably effective. If you're the active type, you can go for a walk or ride a bike.

Listen to soft music – You can do this while sitting and relaxing or doing light tasks, like folding laundry. The music should be soothing. Preferably, the music should only be instrumental. Lyrics can be distracting.

Again, these are just a few ideas. Review the tips presented earlier for raising positive vibrations and clearing negative energy. You will find some of those ideas helpful in achieving a meditative state.

The following meditation is one that I composed to help you activate your chakras and achieve a receptive state that will enhance your ability to communicate with your angels and heighten your psychic senses. You can download a complimentary copy of the audio version of this guided meditation by registering on my website, www. MariaGMaas.com.

A Guided Meditation to Help You Connect with Your Angels

Imagine that it is a warm, sunny day. The weather is picture-perfect. There is a gentle breeze. You are walking along a small, wooded path. Up ahead, there's a clearing that leads to a wooden boardwalk. As you approach the boardwalk, you hear the distant cries of the seagulls.

As you step upon the boardwalk, you now can hear the ocean waves crashing gently along the shoreline just ahead. You can smell the salt air. You can hear the wooden boards beneath your feet creek with every few steps that you take. As you come to the end of the boardwalk, you pause briefly. You listen to the sounds of the ocean waves as they drift back and forth in an easy rhythm. You close your eyes as you lift your face towards the sunlight. You feel the warmth of the sunlight on your face. You feel the gentle breeze move through your hair. You inhale deeply through your nose, drawing in the ocean air. You feel your chest rise slightly as the salty air fills your lungs, holding that breath for a second or two as you imagine it cleansing your aura.

Slowly, you open your eyes exhaling, feeling the breath glide over your lower lip. Now, with your eyes open, admiring the beauty of the sand and sea before you, you take another deep, cleansing breath again, inhaling through your nose, and then, slowing releasing the air through your mouth. One more time…

Drawing the fresh, ocean air in through your nose, and then slowly exhaling through your lips. You feel calm and peaceful, yet at the same time invigorated. There's something so refreshing about the salt air…

You look down at your feet. You remove your sandals and place them at the end of the boardwalk. You place one foot down into the warm sand. Now the next foot… You scrunch your toes once or twice, feeling the warm sand crunch between them. This helps you to feel grounded and connected to Mother Earth. You feel calm, balanced, and connected to all that is good…

Now you are walking barefoot on the warm sand towards the water's edge just a few feet ahead. You begin to feel the sand becoming cooler, then moist. You are now standing on the firm, wet sand. You take just another step or two until you reach the spot where the ocean tide meets the sand. You take one more step forward, and now both feet are standing on the firm, wet sand and you feel the gentle roll of the tide water splashing your toes and the tops of your feet for a moment, then the water recedes back. As the ocean water rolls forward and back, splashing your feet, and then receding again. You stand still, taking in all of the beauty around you. You feel a sense of peace and contentment. You feel connected to the Earth, nature, and the universe. You feel connected to Source. You feel safe. All is well…

Now, as you look down at your feet, you notice the water is beginning to sparkle. Silvery-white sparkles begin to turn brighter and become a white light. You notice that the light is coming from the sky and its reflection is what is causing the shimmering sparkles on the water. You feel safe in the presence of the white light. You know that this white light contains the love and light of your Divine Creator and the Angelic Kingdom. This energy of this loving white light now surrounds you like a protective eggshell. It's as though you're looking out from the inside of a snow globe. You feel so safe and calm yet energized at the same time.

The luminous, white light now begins to take on a ruby-red glow. You notice that the glowing light is still enveloping you. You know you are safe. You enjoy the moment. The warm glow of red soon transforms to orange and you feel vibrant, so alive...the orange light now transforms into a bright yellow glow all around you, you feel so happy at this moment...the light begins to take on an emerald green hue and you feel healthy and loved...the green light becomes infused with blue and now you are bathed in a lovely, sky-blue and you feel so at ease, so calm, although you are silent, you know that you can speak whatever it is that you need to say...just then, the sky-blue glow turns into a deep shade of indigo and you sense your ability to see clearly whatever it is that you need to know in your mind's eye...the indigo light now fades into a lovely shade of violet and you know that you're a spiritual being, having a human experience, and with that you know that your Divine Creator and His Angels have much compassion for you and that they want to assist you in accessing spiritual insight, intuition, and Divine wisdom...the violet shade of the light now begins to fade, returning to a luminous white glow and you are aware now that although you are in a human body, you can connect to your higher self again at anytime you choose...It has always been there for you and your Divine Creator has given you the free will to connect to it at any time you desire to do so.

The light now fades into the atmosphere around you. You are fully aware of your surroundings and feel a sense of well-being. You know that you are open to Divine guidance at will and that this Divine guidance shall be in the highest good of all concerned.

You now make your way back to the wooden boardwalk. When you reach the boardwalk, you brush off the sand on your feet and step into your sandals. You walk back across the boardwalk. Just ahead you see the wooded path that you will take which will lead you back to where you can continue your life's journey. Angel blessings...

After completing a meditation such as this one, you should now find that you are more open and receptive to receiving the messages that your angels have to give you. You can shorten it when necessary. Sometimes you will want to open up to receive messages but need to do it more quickly. We shouldn't rush through our meditation, but we can use one that isn't quite as detailed.

A Review of Essential Things to Do BEFORE Performing a Reading or Healing Session:

1 - Say a prayer of protection for both yourself and your client.
2 - Relax and raise your vibrational energy to communicate with your angels.
3 - Your aura can absorb unwanted energies as you go about your daily personal life. Cleanse and balance your chakras from time to time to remove any blockages caused by leftover psychic debris that you may have absorbed.

Exercise #3

Research guided meditations or write your own to help you connect with your angels. Write the titles and links to any you find here, or use the space to compose your own.

<u>Your Notes</u>:

How Do the Angels Communicate with Us?

We have heard stories of angels appearing as giant winged creatures with echoing voices enveloped in intense light. Appearing in that manner would be scary for many of us, so the angels will most likely not appear to us in that way. The angels I teach you to work with are on a mission by God to assist humanity. They will commonly use a much softer approach and attempt to lead us to harmony for our highest good, not interfering with our free will.

The angels will often give us messages in a way that we are most likely to take notice of and understand. Our angels are aware of how we, as individuals, can best perceive and receive angelic guidance. The angels will use our physical and psychic senses to communicate a message. Physically, they might have us meet the right person or come across the right opportunity at the right time – we call this Divine timing. Psychically, the angels might give us a feeling, a sense of knowing, a visual image, whisper a few succinct words directly to us, have us overhear a meaningful conversation, or put a specific thought or idea in our minds.

Angels will communicate with us by sending signs to tell us they have heard our requests. These signs may come in the form of a song that plays on the radio with lyrics that are especially meaningful to us on a personal level at that very moment (Divine timing). On more than one occasion, I have received messages from my guardian angel and departed loved ones in this way.

One such message stands out very clearly in my mind to this day. In February 2016, I lost my only brother, Louis. We were very close, and I was overwhelmed with grief. While driving in my car, I couldn't stop thinking about him and could barely see where I was going through the well of tears filling my eyes. I suddenly felt compelled to turn on the radio, so I did. The song that had just come on was "Dream On" by Aerosmith. It was a song that I liked, but the lyrics had not ever touched me before as they did at that very moment. I felt like Louis was talking directly to me, and I felt a bit better as it reassured me that my brother was trying to reach out to me from the spirit world to let me know he was aware of what I was going through. Louis sent me a sign so I wouldn't doubt that he was still there with me.

Another sign from our angels may be a feather or a coin lying on the ground directly in our path. We might glance at the clock on the mantle or a license plate on a car just ahead of us, and it displays an angel number (to be discussed in more detail later in this book), like 11:11 or 444. The point here is that angelic communication is usually very subtle and easily missed. Thank God the angels are aware of this, so they will often repeat their messages at least three times to gain our attention.

Some of us might experience hearing a voice that almost sounds like it's coming from within us. This voice will be calm and direct. It will be just a few words that are brief and to the point. It will be a positive and reassuring statement that is protective or helpful. It will always feel loving and supportive. This voice may come to us while asleep in our dream state or wide awake. Sometimes, it may even wake us out of our sleep.

Angels often project thoughts or ideas onto us. We may or may not receive images in our mind's eye along with these thoughts. It usually takes place while thinking about nothing in particular. For example, while doing mundane tasks like combing your hair, loading the dishwasher, folding clothes, etc., you suddenly know the answer to a pressing question. In many cases, it will be like one of those so-called "light-bulb moments."

What are the 4 Major Clairs?

The term "clairs" is derived from the prefix of the following words and is an abbreviation used for referencing all of the following terms that define the different modes of psychic perceptivity: *clairvoyance*/clear seeing, *clairaudience*/ clear hearing, *clairsentience*/clear feeling, and *claircognizance*/ clear knowing. These are the psychic senses, and we may have one or more that work well for us. If you are *claircognizant*, you somehow seem to know things and are not exactly sure how you know them; there's likewise a good chance you will find that you also receive and perceive messages through any or all of the other *clairs* too. There are more clairs, but these four are the most common ones.

What are Your Strongest Clairs?

There are quizzes you can take and experiments that you can try to test your psychic senses. You can search the Internet for them or find them in books on the subject. The teacher in me tells me that an excellent way to find out what your predominant *clairs* are is to consider your learning style. Are you a visual, auditory, or kinesthetic (hands-on) learner?

Here's an example: If you prefer to be shown how to do something and like to see illustrations when reading instructions, then you are a visual learner. In this case, your predominant *clair* is likely *clairvoyance*, i.e., clear seeing. As a *clairvoyant*, you will find that you will often be able to receive and perceive angelic guidance that is visual. The angels will probably send you images in your mind's eye or draw your attention to look at something at the right moment that will have meaning for you.

If you are an auditory learner, you like hearing things explained to you. You are probably clairaudient. In this case, your angels will most likely try to whisper in your ear. For example, you may hear a few succinct words. You may hear your angel speak to you in a dream. You may also overhear a conversation that will convey a message to you. The angels can orchestrate for you to be in the right place at the right time to hear what you need.

If you are a kinesthetic (hands-on) learner, you will get feelings about things. You are most likely empathic, and the angels will send you sensations to get your attention and to help you understand a message. In this case, you are *clairsentient*.

Many people will find that they get messages in more than one way. Sometimes you may know something. An idea pops into your head, and it's what you need to know, but interestingly, it comes at a moment when you weren't thinking about the situation; it just comes to you seemingly from out-of-the-blue. In this case, you're probably *claircognizant*.

Over time, how you receive and perceive messages from your angels, spirit guides, or departed loved ones will change. It may or may not happen, but if it does, don't worry about it. Just go with the flow.

I suggest just paying attention to what you get when you get it. Keep a journal of insights as you receive them. As you continue working with your angels, this will help you to fine-tune your communication with them.

Is There a Difference Between Intuition and Psychic Ability?

There is a definite difference between intuition and psychic ability. I base this on the reasoning that intuition comes from within, and psychic ability comes from an external source. Intuition kicks in automatically when needed. Very often, intuition occurs when we're focused on or are in a situation that calls for intuitive guidance. In contrast, psychic experiences can come unexpectedly and, at times, without instigation on the part of the psychic.

Intuition. Intuition is your soul's "GPS." Unlike the GPS in your motor vehicle that speaks in loud and distinct commands, the voice of your intuition is usually very subtle. It's more like an inner knowing that suggests you turn right instead of left or may say, "Yes, go ahead. It will be good for you." Other times a thought will come saying, "That's not a good idea... Be careful..." Then there are times when it's a feeling deep in your gut that makes you apprehensive or even a bit sick to your stomach about whatever it is you're considering. Most people will agree that they've had such experiences. They're not at all uncommon. It's nature's way of keeping you safe. It could be your guardian angel nudging you or your own life experience that your subconscious brings to the surface when essential.

Your guardian angel was assigned to you by God and given the power to speak to you through your intuition. Some people have a stronger instinct than others and are more innately attuned to the world around them. Be assured that this doesn't just happen by itself. It's because they've paid attention to it and continue to exercise it. The good news is that everybody has intuition, and the more you understand and use it, the stronger it will become for you.

An Example of Using Intuition in a Reading:

An intuitive tarot reader might get a feeling about which cards in a spread are the most relevant for the sitter and spend more time discussing those cards than other cards in the reading. That same reader might get an overall gut feeling about whether the situation that the sitter inquired about is going to work out in the way that they hope it will. The feeling is coming from within the reader. It is an inner sense they need to focus on certain cards in the spread.

Psychic Ability. My understanding of psychic ability is that it is distinguishable from intuition. Psychic ability can be considered an antenna that can tune into various frequencies outside yourself. The information a psychic can tap into is not from within them like their intuition; it's coming from some outside source. That external source can be another living person, an angel, a spirit guide, or a departed soul. Sometimes it's similar to intuition, but the main difference is that it's not coming from within the subconscious mind but from another source that's not part of you. Psychic ability will manifest through the four major clairs, as defined earlier.

Telepathy occurs in people with powerful, intuitive abilities who are likely psychic. They may or may not realize it. Unlike our intuition that kicks in when we're in a situation or focusing on something, or via telepathy that we may have with those we have close relationships with, psychic experiences can pop up out of nowhere, or they can be tuned into on-demand by a skilled psychic. You can likely develop your psychic abilities if your intuition is this strong. Telepathy is often the bridge that leads one to explore their psychic abilities; however, some may not take that next step.

Psychic ability is a genetic faculty. For example, if you have musical ability and can sing or play an instrument, that is an ability that you are born with, and there are likely to be others in your family with a similar talent. Although you can further develop this skill with practice, there are varying degrees to which you can expand it.

An Example of Using Psychic Ability in a Reading:

A psychic tarot reader might get a clear picture they see in their mind of something that has nothing to do with the cards in the spread nor the question asked by their client. The psychic explains the image they see, and their client understands it. The vision the psychic describes to their client would have significance to the client even if the psychic couldn't interpret the meaning of it at the time. In this scenario, the psychic's vision comes from an external source.

How to Use Your Intuition to Make Better Decisions

An excellent way to judge whether something is right for us is to pay close attention to how a particular choice or plan of action makes us feel. Our intuition not only warns us about things to avoid but also urges us to carry on with the things that are right for us.

Let's look at an example through a fictitious scenario:

Suppose you just received an offer from your employer giving you the option of a promotion if you are willing to relocate. The new position that's become available is one that you are qualified for and will also significantly increase your current annual salary. You would need to relocate to a region you have visited many times since you already have friends and family living there. You also have friends and family near where you are living right now. Your only concern is that you are happy where you live now, and moving is stressful.

To make this decision, you call upon the angels for assistance. Here's an example of how that would work:

You call upon Archangel Michael and your guardian angel (it's not essential to know the name of your guardian angel). You ask Archangel Michael to protect your aura and ensure that you intuitively receive only that which is in your highest good. You ask your guardian angel to help you to accurately perceive, through your sense of intuition, the guidance for this critical decision that is in your highest good.

First, you consider your <u>current</u> position and location. You ask yourself, "What does it look like, smell like, taste like, and sound like?" Pay close attention to how you feel. Do you feel calm or edgy? Does it feel right? You make notes about what you experienced in your journal. You repeat this process over the next few days and record the experience in your journal.

Next, you consider the <u>new</u> position and location. Again, you ask yourself, "What does it look like, smell like, taste like, and sound like?" You pay close attention to how you feel. Do you feel calm or edgy? Does it feel right? You make notes about what you experienced in your journal. Repeat this process over the next few days and record the experience in your journal.

After doing this at least three times for each option, you review the notes in your journal. You now have a clear and confident feeling about your best option.

If you are still undecided at this point and have the time to wait before making your decision, you ask Archangel Michael and your guardian angel to help you release any worries or concerns to them. You let it go and try not to think about it for a few more days or weeks, after which you repeat the entire process. You are now able to make your decision with confidence.

Note: You can easily modify this exercise to help you use your intuition to make other types of decisions with the guidance of your angels.

Connecting with Your Guardian Angel

Everyone has a guardian angel. Some believe that we have more than one. Unlike archangels, whom God created to assist all of humanity, God made a special guardian angel just for each one of us. Our guardian angels know our soul's purpose and work very hard to guide us so that we may fulfill it. During one of my meditation sessions, the angels told me our guardian angels were with us throughout our past incarnations and would remain with us through our current and future lives.

Although, as a child, I remember learning that our guardian angel is with us from conception to our physical death, I now know otherwise. I know that my guardian angel has been with me throughout my past lives and will remain with me until my soul has learned all the lessons it needs to learn, no matter how many lifetimes it might take to accomplish. I trust in what the angels have told me.

Connecting with your guardian angel is easy. Your guardian angel wants to communicate with you as much as you want to connect with it. Like all other angels, your guardian angel is pure spirit and does not have a physical body; however, you may perceive your guardian angel as a male, or a female based on the energy radiated by the angel. Although your guardian angel does not have a gender, some angels' energies will feel more feminine, and others will feel more masculine.

You can connect with your guardian angel through prayer, meditation, and dreams. Prayer sets the stage and prepares you to be open to your guardian angel's guidance. It also helps to protect you and ensure that your guardian angel will come through for you and that some lower entity will not trick you. It needn't be an elaborate prayer; a few simple words will suffice. Here's a short and simple prayer that I wrote:

> *Dear Guardian Angel, so strong and bright,*
> *infused with God's wisdom, love, and light,*
> *Guardian Angel, please stand beside me,*
> *Guardian Angel, protect and guide me.*

After you say your prayer, ask your guardian angel for guidance. Visualize a bright, golden light filling up the room. Feel comforted in knowing that your guardian angel is with you right now. Please note that you can follow this procedure by writing a letter to your guardian angel.

Your guardian angel loves you unconditionally and wants to help you in any way that is in God's will and your own free will. Trust that you will receive an answer. You may get a response immediately; however, it may take some time. Thank your guardian angel for the guidance you have received or are open to receiving. Pay attention to the signs your guardian angel gave you, as we discussed earlier in the section titled "How do the Angels Communicate with Us?"

Keep a journal of the questions you ask your guardian angel and note the messages you receive in response to those questions. Note how you received the messages, i.e., whether it was something you could see, hear, feel, or know. The more detail you can record, the more in touch you will become with how you receive messages.

Exercise #4

Follow the steps in the previous section to connect with your guardian angel. You can ask your guardian angel a general question or specific question. Make notes about how you received or perceived the message. Did you see, hear, feel, or know your guardian angel's answer? Write whatever message you receive in your journal. You may also use the space below to describe your experience.

<u>Your Notes</u>:

Using Guided Meditations to Receive Guidance from Your Guardian Angel

Guided meditations are an excellent way to connect with your guardian angel. Stay positive if you first find that you don't receive a message. With faith and practice, you will receive angel messages. Be patient with yourself. Just enjoy the process. If you practice relaxing and enjoying the meditation experience, this will help to quiet your ego and, in turn, help you be more receptive to your guardian angel's guidance.

Does Your Guardian Angel have a Name?

Your guardian angel doesn't have a name, and you should not make up a name for your guardian angel. However, your guardian angel may provide a name you can call it if you ask it for one.

Should your guardian angel choose a name to share with you, look up the meaning of the name. Please note that the name your guardian gives you to call it by might not end in "el," like the archangels — any title, from a common name to something unique, might be spoken. The name shared will have a particular association with you. It's a name you will feel akin to, and the meaning of the name's origin is likely to resonate with you on a deeper level. If you look up the meaning of the name and its origin, you will most likely be amazed at its significance to you on a personal level. If you look up the numerology of the name, you are also likely to find that it's meaningful to you as well.

Getting to Know Your Guardian Angel - A Guided Meditation

I wrote and recorded a guided meditation titled "Getting to Know Your Guardian Angel." Find a comfortable place to sit where you won't be disturbed. You can download the audio of this recording as a complimentary gift when you register as a member of my website, MariaGMaas.com. The following text is a transcript of that guided meditation:

Let's get ready to begin... Sit in a comfortable chair... Your arms and legs should not be crossed... Place your hands palm-side down on your lap... Your feet should be resting flat on the floor, give yourself permission to take this time for you...

Relax your arms, wrists and hands, relax your shoulders, release any tension from your neck and spine, relax your torso, relax your legs, relax your feet and toes...

Now close your eyes... Take a deep cleansing breath in through your nose... Feel your chest rise slowly as you inhale... Imagine that this breath is drawing in energy from Mother Earth... This energy is gently removing any energetic blockages from your aura making it easier for you to communicate with your guardian angel.

As you inhale, visualize this energy as a white light. This white light sparkles as you draw it up through your spine and through the top of your head. As you exhale, visualize any blockages along its path that may have caused interference with your guardian angel's messages for you being eliminated.

Keeping your eyes closed, inhale and exhale 2 more times in the same manner to ensure that there is no residue from any blockages remaining behind…

Now that all blockages have been cleared, in your mind's eye, you see that there is a golden light about arm's length in distance above your head. You feel warmth radiating from this light that makes you feel very safe and calm. You recognize this golden light as your guardian angel… You feel your guardians angel's love and compassion for you.

Now, consciously send gratitude to your guardian angel for always being here for you… Thank your guardian angel for its loving guidance and assistance for your highest good. Thank your guardian angel for not judging you… Thank your guardian angel for respecting your God-given free will…

The golden light now beings to shimmer with a delicate radiance… This is your guardian angel reflecting its acknowledgment of your gratitude. Your guardian angel accepts your appreciation because it knows that you are now open to its loving guidance and assistance and that this is what God wants for you. Now your *guardian angel knows that you have just given it permission to do the work that God created it to do – and that is to be your at your side, helping you to achieve your soul's purpose.*

The golden light shimmers even brighter as it draws closer to you now… You feel so warm, so safe, so loved… You feel a tingling sensation along the crown of your head… This is your energy now linking with your guardian angel's energy… Your vibrational energy is now high enough to connect with your guardian angel…

You now ask your guardian angel to draw even closer… You feel the warm and loving energy wash down over you, blending with your aura… Your senses are heightened… You are now open to see, hear, feel, or know whatever you need to know that's in your highest good…

Ask your guardian angel a question now… You can ask it for guidance on something specific, you can ask it its name, you can ask it for protection, you can ask it for just a general message… Ask your question now and pay attention to anything that you may see, hear, feel, smell, taste, or just know…

Now that you've had a few minutes to connect with your guardian angel, keep in mind whatever you may have experienced… Allow your guardian angels golden light and energy to slowly fade from your aura… Know that your guardian angel is always close by, and you can connect with it again at any time you choose…

You can now begin to wiggle your toes and your fingers… Feel the chair that you are seated in, feel the floor beneath your feet. Slowly, open your eyes… You are awake, alert, and energized. You can easily recall your experience…

After completing this guided meditation, make a note of anything that you experienced. Don't feel frustrated if you ask for a specific message or your guardian angel's name and an answer doesn't come to you. You may be trying too hard. When you are ready, try it again, and be sure not to force anything. Focus on relaxing and enjoying the experience. It's essential to be able to relax and clear your mind.

Receiving Angelic Guidance through Dreams

Dreams are an excellent way to receive guidance from your angels. Your angels can appear to you visually in your dreams or send you messages telepathically. You may recall the dream, or you may not. Even if you don't remember the dream, trust that you received your angel's guidance in your subconscious. When you are asleep, your ego is on pause, making it easier to receive suggestions from your angels.

If you would like your guardian angel to communicate with you in this way more often, when you go to bed at night, ask your guardian angel to speak to you during your sleep. Request that upon waking, you recall the dream and store the guidance within your subconscious, so it is available to you when you need it. Ask that the advice you receive is always for your highest good.

Is it Just a Dream or an Angel Message?

Dreams have significance in the real world. Dreams are a symbolic language, and the images in dreams tend to contain hidden meanings and messages. When analyzing and interpreting dreams, it is essential to understand that the stories told in dreams are symbolic and not meant to be literal. The significance of dreams for each dreamer is a personal matter related to each person's experience and emotions.

However, some do experience precognitive dreams. Precognitive dreams are a type of prophetic dream. They inform or warn you about something that has yet to occur. I have these kinds of dreams from time to time. I can tell the difference between a precognitive dream and an ordinary dream because this kind of dream makes such an impression on me that I can recall it in detail. It is a dream that I will not forget for years to come.

For example, I once had a precognitive dream about a young woman I worked with years ago. In the dream, I saw her driving her car to work. I saw it was snowing in the dream, and the roads were treacherous. She was going too fast and lost control of her vehicle. She was in a horrific accident, and I feared that it would leave her young son without a mother or a mother who would no longer be physically able to care for him.

This dream was alarming, and I could not stop thinking about it. I kept it to myself for a few days, but I decided to tell this woman about my dream because I believed telling her could keep her out of harm's way. I didn't tell her all the grave details, but I did tell her enough of the dream so that she would drive more defensively.

A few weeks later, on a snowy morning, she remembered my dream as she was driving to work and was driving extra cautiously. As she traveled down the winding, snow-covered road near our workplace, another car in front of her lost control. It spun around and crashed into a tree. She attempted to avoid it but could not. Her car was totaled, but thankfully, she was unharmed. It could have been much worse for her if she had not been extra cautious that morning.

I credit the positive outcome of this event to both my guardian angel and hers. Our guardian angels speak to us during our dreams. They can communicate with us as well as each other when necessary.

The Difference Between Angels and Spirit Guides

While angels can be considered spirit guides, spirit guides should not be regarded as angels. Angels are God's messengers. They are pure love and light emanating from God; hence, the archangels' names end in "el," meaning "of God." Angels have never lived an earthly life, whereas spirit guides have usually lived as human beings. Spirit guides can be a departed loved one, another soul you knew in a past life, another soul you never met who lived during another time, some other evolved being, or even an ascended master.

Spirit guides come into our lives to assist us with anything from the mundane to the spiritual. Spirit guides can help us with parenting, teaching, learning, public speaking, writing, artwork, psychic work, mediumship, tarot reading, and much more. As we learn and grow, different spirit guides will come and go to assist us on our journeys.

Communicating with your spirit guide is a similar process as is, communicating with angels. Be aware of how angels and spirit guides communicate and pay attention to the signs you receive. Always begin by grounding and shielding before you proceed with your request for guidance.

Who are the Archangels?

The archangels are governing angels. God has employed the archangels to oversee all other angels. Along with this task, God has granted each archangel a specialty with which to assist and serve humanity. The archangels have specific names all ending with the suffix, "el". El is one of the names for God and is a word that is Hebrew in origin, derived from the longer variation, "Elohim." El is also said to mean "might" or "mighty".

Each archangel's name (except for Metatron and Sandalphon) ends in "el" because they are of God. Metatron and Sandalphon do not end in "el." This is because they are the only two archangels that were not created as angels. They were human prophets by the names of Enoch and Elijah, respectively. It is believed by many that these two prophets led such exemplary lives, that they were accepted into the angelic realm so that they could continue serving God and humanity.

No one knows how many archangels God created. Some religious traditions say that there are seven, while others disagree. From what I've studied, the four archangels acknowledged most often are Archangels Michael, Gabriel, Raphael, and Uriel. I believe that the number of archangels is unlimited and still growing. I also believe that God creates archangels as needed and that some lower-ranking angels become elevated to the rank of an archangel.

The following chart contains the names of 15 archangels, the meanings of their names, and the specialties for which they are most well known:

Reference Chart of 15 Archangels

ARCHANGEL	MEANING OF NAME	SPECIALTY
Ariel	*Lion/Lioness of God*	**Courage, manifesting, abundance, prosperity, leadership, protection and healing of animals.** Assists us in having the courage we need to manifest our dreams into reality, inspires philanthropy, encourages and supports environmentalism and animal rights.
Azrael	*Whom God Helps*	**Peaceful transition of newly departed souls and comforts the grieving, supports counselors, promotes compassion and empathy.** Ensures a peaceful transition at the time of death and heals grief, supports grief counselors in their work, eases fears associated with death and dying.
Chamuel	*Eyes of God*	**Finding whatever you seek or need, seeing the big picture, balancing the heart chakra.** Sometimes this archangel is called Camael. AA Chamuel can help you find anything from a lost set of car keys, a new career, your soul mate, or even peace of mind – nothing is too big or too small.

Gabriel	*Strength of God*	**Communication, Motivation, Nurturing, Inspiration, Creativity.** Sometimes called Gabrielle, this archangel is known as the patron saint of parents or those who want to become parents. He/she has a softer energy so may be perceived as feminine. Gabriel is named in the Bible for announcing to the Virgin Mary, she was to conceive the Son of God and name Him, "Jesus," meaning, "Savior." He is also known as *the messenger angel* and helps those in the field of public speaking. AA Gabriel also assists painters, writers, and teachers. He is often depicted blowing a horn.
Haniel	*Grace of God*	**Healing emotional issues, fortitude, women's issues, and honing psychic abilities and/or mediumship.** Also known as *Glory of God*. Haniel can assist in overcoming difficulties. Very connected with the moon, cycles of nature, and the female body, and receptiveness to the spirit world.
Jeremiel	*Mercy of God*	**Keeper of karmic contracts, defender of the wounded healers, inner strength, supervisor of life reviews, prophecy and past life recall through dreams.** Also known as Ramiel, the *Angel of Hope*. Assists the living and newly departed souls with life reviews, helps to clear negative karma and earn positive karma, aids in the understanding of Divine order, brings healing through love and compassion.
Jophiel	*Beauty of God*	**Brings out the positive in all situations, raises self-esteem, harmonizes and balances.** Archangel Jophiel helps to raise our vibrational energy, enables us to beautify thoughts and our surroundings, encourages us to commune with and appreciate nature, inspires artists, and promotes self-care.

Metatron	*The Lesser Yahweh (YHVH)*	**Teaching/learning of esoteric wisdom for adults and children, God's sacred scribe, keeper of sacred geometry, operator of time and space.** Archangel Metatron helps you prioritize your goals, assists in speeding up achievement of your life purpose, cleanses and optimizes your chakras for optimum performance, maintains order of the cosmos.
Michael	*He Who is Like God*	**Protection, Courage, Clarity of Thought and Life Purpose.** He is probably the most well-known archangel. In Christianity, he is referred to as Saint Michael, the Archangel. He is the patron saint of police officers, military personnel, and rescue workers. Michael is named in the Bible and is known for banishing fallen angels from Heaven; therefore, Michael is known as the warrior angel. He is often depicted holding a shield and/or flaming sword.
Raguel	*Friend of God*	**Harmonious relationships, Divine timing, making new friends, promoting fair and just outcomes.** Encourages peace and harmony in all relationships – friends, lovers, coworkers, etc. Assists in meeting the right people – soul mate relationships, being in the right place at the right time for your highest good, rectifies wrongdoing with just action, a great angel to call upon when making contractual agreements to ensure fairness.
Raphael	*Healing of God*	**Physical, mental, emotional, and spiritual healing, protection in long distance travel.** The archangel who assists healers in doing their work. He can help you find the right doctor, dentist, or therapist. He can help heal relationships too. In Christianity, he is known as, Saint Raphael, the Archangel and is mentioned by name in the Book of Tobit.

Raziel	Secrets of God	**Insight, intuition, spiritual wisdom, clairvoyance, interpretation of esoteric symbolism, divination, manifesting, remembering and/or healing past life issues.** Very high ranking and esteemed archangel. Sits so close to the throne of God, it's believed that he knows the Divine secrets of the Heavens. Works closely with those who seek higher levels of enlightenment in the attempt to bridge science and spirituality.
Sandalphon	*Soul Brother/Co-brother*	**Carry prayers to Heaven, protection of unborn children, encourages gentleness and loyalty, inspires musicians.** Known as the "twin brother" of Metatron because Sandalphon originated as the human prophet called, Elijah. Like Metatron his name does not end in "el" and he was accepted into the angelic kingdom for leading such a pious life. Call upon him to help enhance your communication with God.
Uriel	*Light of God* or *Fire of God*	**Showing us the way, lighting our path, knowledge, wisdom.** He is often depicted holding a lantern. His light shines to lead us through the darkness. He assists those who have lost their way. He is known as the "intellectual angel" and assists us with studying and learning. Uriel is also the archangel of bright ideas.
Zadkiel	*Righteousness of God*	**Compassion, forgiveness, finding truth, self-transformation, connects seen and unseen, promotes knowledge and understanding.** Teaches us to trust in the benevolence of God, assists in the retention of useful knowledge gained from current and past lives, helps to release negative memories from both current and past lives, and brings comfort in our hour of need.

ANGELIC RAYS

The concept of angelic rays or colors is not widely recognized or studied in mainstream Christianity or other Abrahamic religions. The angelic rays are part of the visible white light spectrum. These are the seven colors of the rainbow and are associated with the seven main chakras, including the 8th Chakra/Soul-star Chakra.

In the following chart, we will discuss the seven powerful archangels, corresponding chakras, and colors of the light rays within which each of these archangel's Divine assistance activates.

Angelic Rays Chart

Angelic Ray	Archangel (meaning of name)	Special Focus	Chakra
Ruby-red	Uriel – *Light/Fire of God*	Illuminating the path, helping to ease fear, feel secure and confident, get back on the right path, remember facts, inspiring the intellect, releasing deep-seated energy blocks	Root or Base
Orange	Gabriel – *Strength of God*	Nurturing, creativity, motivation, inspiration, originality, being yourself, verbal or written communication, stress relief, conception, birth, parenting, teaching, public speaking	Sacral
Yellow	Jophiel – *Beauty of God*	Uplifting spirits, raising vibrations or keeping vibration high, feeling joyful, boosting self-esteem, wisdom, mental clarity, communing with nature and animals, connecting to the higher self/Holy Spirit, connecting to angels and spirit guides	Solar Plexus
Green	Raphael – *Healing of God*	Healing of any kind – physical, mental, or emotional…protection for long-distance travelers – air, land, or sea, and astral traveling…balance, harmony, ability to love unconditionally (others as well as oneself)	Heart
Blue	Michael – *He Who is Like God*	Protection, clearing negativity, courage, mental clarity, cord-cutting, communication, quieting the ego, bolstering faith, seeking a higher truth, speaking your truth, deepening devotion to God	Throat

Indigo	Raziel – *Secrets of God*	Insight, intuition, spiritual wisdom, manifesting, activating all the *Clairs*, especially, clairvoyance and claircognizance, telepathic abilities, ESP, psychic abilities, cosmic awareness, remembering and healing blocks from past lives, accessing Akashic records, accuracy in interpreting esoteric symbols like in the tarot or even dreams, Divine enlightenment	Third Eye
Violet	Zadkiel – Righteousness *of God*	Guardian of the Gateway to Your Higher Self/Holy Spirit, Divine compassion, calms emotions, recovery from addictions, ease addictive tendencies, embrace forgiveness of self and others, enhances meditation, psychic visions, and ability to communicate with angels and departed loved ones in dreams, improving memory, aids in learning and teaching, accessing past lives, releasing karmic debt, earning good karma, healer of mind, body, and soul	Crown
White	Metatron – *The Lesser Yahweh (YHVH)*	"Light body activation" – that is, accessing key information through your higher self/Holy Spirit, "ascension into cosmic consciousness," enlightenment, cleanse, balance, and align all 7 main chakras, organization, motivation, prioritization, bend time and space, speed up or slow down, spiritual evolution.	Soul Star

How to Discern if It's Angelic Guidance that You're Receiving

One of the surest ways to know if the guidance you are receiving is coming from the angels is always to follow the ritual of grounding and shielding. Calling upon Archangel Michael to preside over your readings and meditations will ensure that only messages of love, light, and Divine wisdom come through. As an example, I always call upon Archangel Michael. I ask Archangel Michael for his protection in the name of Jesus. I may call upon Mother Mary as well. For extra security, you can also request the protection of another loving and benevolent ascended master you trust.

Following this type of ritual before requesting angelic guidance will help you feel safer and reassured that the messages you receive are indeed from God's loving angels. It will help quiet your mind, so you are more peaceful and relaxed. It also makes it easier for the angels to communicate with you.

Once you have prepared yourself in this manner, you will find that the messages will begin to flow with ease and grace. You will be able to see, hear, feel, or know whatever it is that you need to know for your highest good or for someone else who is open to receiving a message from the angels through you.

The message will always be kind, supportive, and helpful. It will never invoke fear or suggest anything that would cause harm to anyone. It will never make you or the other person receiving the message through you feel uneasy, uncomfortable, fearful, angry, or depressed. If that should happen, stop immediately and consult a mental health professional. A clergy member, such as a priest, rabbi, or pastor, may also be able to offer further assistance.

Angelic guidance promotes a beautiful sense of well-being. You will feel safe, loved, and supported by receiving Divine guidance. Angelic guidance will help you to know that you are never alone. It will give you inspiration and motivation, along with the steps you need to take to move you in the right direction to achieve your soul's destiny.

Working with the Angel Oracle Cards

An angel oracle deck is an easy, safe, and excellent tool for receiving angelic guidance, especially when new to this type of work. The essential thing to know is that it is optional to use angel oracle cards, or any other tools for that matter, to communicate with your angels. You and the angels are all that is needed.

Communication involves exchanging thoughts, ideas, knowledge, and so on between two or more people. It can transpire in person, where each person takes a turn speaking and listening. Communication also occurs through tools to exchange writing, images, or sound. Sometimes there may be physical contact, like a handshake or a pat on the back. Other times a simple facial expression or hand gesture will suffice. Some people also can communicate with others telepathically, that is, through thoughts only.

Angelic communication isn't any different. If you can communicate with another human being in any of the previously described ways, you can also communicate with your angels. All of these communication techniques can work for you. You only need to set your intention to open up the lines of communication with your angels. The most important thing to remember is that the same things that can break down and block communication between people can also interfere with angelic communication. Combining your knowledge of basic communication skills along with the *Law of Vibration* and the *Law of Attraction* will be like adding an amplifier to your telephone or upgrading your telecommunication service to a premium, higher-speed service!

Now, getting back to the angel oracle cards... Although it's not necessary to use cards to receive angelic guidance, it's proven to be a very effective means for most people to attain the Divine guidance or inspiration they seek. The cards satisfy our need for something tangible while, at the same time, giving us something attractive to look at and providing a means of focus.

Angel oracle cards have become very popular. There are so many beautiful decks to choose from, which can become overwhelming. So that is one of the reasons I recommend The *Angelic View Oracle Cards* deck for you. The deck comes with a complimentary guidebook and journal that you can download. Visit my website, MariaGMaas.com, for more information.

Preparing Your Deck for Use – Consecrating, clearing, and blessing your deck(s)

If your deck is new, you should consecrate it and make it your own. Hold the deck in one hand or lay the deck on the table and turn over each card one at a time. Touch every card in the deck. As you do this, ask Archangels Michael and Raziel to make this deck a clear and accurate tool for angel messages and to help you accurately interpret the cards' meanings for the highest good of all concerned.

Every time you pose a new question, you should clear the deck. Whether your deck is brand new, or you've used it many times before, you should clear it before every reading because the cards absorb energy. Even if it has just been you handling the cards (by the way, whether to let someone else touch your cards is entirely up to you), they can hold onto energy from previous questions, and it only takes a second or two to clear it, so do it quite often.

Clearing your deck is simple to do. Hold the deck in your non-dominant hand, so if you are right-handed, hold the deck in your left hand and vice-versa. Hold the deck face down with the card's back design facing you. Make a fist with your dominant hand, knock once firmly on the top of the deck with the back design of the cards facing up towards you, and say, "Clear" aloud or silently to yourself. Visualize the remnants of energy left behind in the deck from the previous reading being neutralized immediately. Sometimes I like to blow on my deck as I say, "Clear!" silently to myself and visualize the deck's energy being cleared and neutralized.

Next, you should bless the deck. Hold the deck face down in the palm of your non-dominant hand and place your dominant hand's palm down on the top so that your palm is covering the deck's back design. Do this before every reading. Say a prayer something like this:

> *Dear Archangels Michael & Raziel (or insert another specific archangel's name if you feel drawn to do so),*
>
> *Please bless this deck. Infuse it with love, light, and Divine wisdom that will always be for the highest good of all concerned. Please help me to accurately interpret the messages you bring forth through these cards now and always.*
>
> *[I ask this in Jesus' name. Amen.] The text in brackets is optional based on your religious beliefs. You can modify or eliminate this line.*

How to Conduct an Angel Oracle Card Reading for Yourself or Someone Else

There isn't very much difference between doing a reading for yourself or someone else when using angel oracle cards. You may find it easier to do a reading for another person than for yourself, especially if you are using tarot cards or some other type of oracle. When we do a reading for someone else, it is easier to be objective. When reading for yourself, you need to be flexible about the outcome. You need to be completely open to receiving guidance, even if it's not what you want to hear.

The great thing about using angel oracle cards like *The Angelic View Oracle Cards* is that all the messages are positive and uplifting, making the guidance easier to take, even if it means that we need to make a shift in our thinking. Messages from our angels are always loving, healing, inspirational, and empowering.

When you begin a reading, always start by setting up sacred space (even if it's as simple as placing a special cloth on the table upon which you plan to lay out your cards). Next, say a prayer of protection. If you have the time, meditate for a few minutes. It's good practice to meditate before doing a reading. If you are reading for a client, you can spend some time in mediation before seeing them.

Now you are ready to clear your deck as described above. After you have cleared your deck, follow that up with a blessing on your deck. Next, you are ready to pose your question to the angels. Your question could be about something specific. Alternatively, you can request a general angel message leaving it up to the angels to respond with whatever is most necessary for you or your client to know. Always ask the angels for the information that comes through to be in the highest good of whoever it concerns, whether that be yourself or your client.

It is good practice to phrase the question in such a way that it is an open-ended question, not a Yes/No question. We request guidance from the angels; we do not ask them to make choices or decisions for us. Remember, angels will never interfere with the will of God or a person's God-given free will. The angels are here to assist us by empowering us to use our best judgment.

Once we have a correctly phrased question, we can determine the number of cards and the layout/spread we will use. Spreads help to set a clear intention of how the angels may respond to our question so that the correct cards land in the right place at the right time. This synchronistic alignment begins to take place as we shuffle the cards. You and your client must concentrate on the question as you shuffle your deck. Just before stating the question, insert the following phrase:

> *Archangels, please allow me to see, hear, feel, or know whatever (person's name) (or I, if the reading is for yourself) need to know most about (insert question) that is in (person's name or my) highest good.*

When you feel like it's time to stop shuffling, or you hear the word "Stop," or you receive another sign from your angels that you've mixed the deck enough, stop shuffling. Trust that the cards will be in the correct order.

Fan the cards out on the table. If you are reading for yourself, use your non-dominant hand (this is your intuitive hand) to draw out the specific number of cards for the spread one by one. If you are reading for someone else, have that person draw the cards in the same manner and pass them to you face up one at a time. Begin to lay out the cards based on the spread you have chosen. The cards should be placed face up. For additional tips, refer to *The Angelic View Oracle Cards Guidebook & Journal* (a free download from my website). I suggest starting with the Single-Card method (described in the guidebook) if you are new to reading cards or unfamiliar with this deck. A wealth of information can be derived from a single card.

Read the card title and printed message on each card, one at a time. It is optional to read them in a particular order. If you feel drawn to a specific card and feel that that is where you want to begin, then start there. Just because you may be using a Past, Present, and Future spread doesn't mean you must first begin reading from the Past position. Just go with the flow.

Consider how the printed message on the card relates to the question. Pay attention to any impressions you receive as you gaze at the card. Notice the colors, shapes, facial expressions, and so on. Let the angels speak to you through your senses. Remember, you asked, "To see, hear, feel, or know..." Try not to overthink. Allow your intuition and psychic senses to work for you. If you are reading for someone else, say what you get, even if you think it doesn't make sense or sounds silly. The person you are reading for will likely understand the message. I cannot express enough how important it is to trust the messages you receive.

Practice, Practice, Practice!

Practice by keeping a journal of your readings. Practice drawing a single card for a general daily message for yourself. Practice drawing a single card for guidance on a particular situation. Record the angel messages you receive in your journal. Once you feel comfortable reading for yourself, you can begin reading for friends and family. After you've received positive feedback and gained confidence in your readings, you should be ready to start doing readings for clients.

Getting Angel Messages from Tarot Cards or Other Oracle Decks

If you are familiar with the tarot, you can use a tarot deck also to receive angel messages. It's all about the intent. You set the stage and connect with the angels you want to communicate with for guidance. You and your client are protected if you follow the process taught in this course— the messages you receive come from a source of God's love and light.

I have had much success receiving very detailed messages by combining tarot cards with angel cards. If you prefer to avoid using a tarot deck, you can combine different angel oracle decks and add more depth to your readings. I often use more than one deck. You can either mix the decks or select certain cards from certain decks putting them together to create a unique deck. I designed *The Angelic View Oracle Cards* the same size as tarot cards so they can easily blend with any standard tarot deck. I often like to have several decks ready to use and intuitively choose one or more of them to draw from as I move on from reading to reading.

When I do readings live on-air on my Internet radio show, *The Angelic View*, I mostly use my deck, *The Angelic View Oracle Cards*. Sometimes, I also use the *Radiant Rider-Waite Tarot* and one or two other oracle decks that I select intuitively from my library of decks. I do this because I enjoy having options. It allows me to use my intuition to pull cards from the decks that I feel drawn to at that moment for the reading. I combine this with my psychic impressions. Sometimes I don't even pull cards because the angels send me a message through one or more of my clairs. As I mentioned, you don't need to use tools or props to do readings. You only need to develop one or more clairs and hone your intuition.

Many readers enjoy working with cards. The cards are beautiful and help to jump-start your intuition. Working with the cards aids in the development of psychic ability. In addition, clients enjoy seeing the cards drawn for them as it adds to the allure of a reading.

You should now have a deeper understanding of how to use angel oracle cards to receive guidance and messages from your angels and the Divine. Always approach your readings with an open mind and a kind heart. Trust that the messages you receive are for you or your client's highest good and will help you on your journey.

As you continue your studies, remember to be patient with yourself and trust the learning process. It takes time and practice to develop a relationship with your angels and to become proficient in conducting readings. So don't worry if you don't get it right away – keep practicing and have fun!

What Are Angel Crystals and How Can You Use Them?

Angel crystals are certain crystals that are naturally attuned to the angelic realm. Angel crystals are beneficial to use during meditation because they can assist you in raising your vibrations to a higher frequency that is more closely aligned with the angelic realm.

You can hold the crystal in your receiving hand, which usually is your non-dominant hand. You can also place the crystal on a table or shelf near your meditation area. I keep mine on a shelf just about a foot above my head where I am seated during my meditation so that it is just above my crown chakra. There isn't a right or wrong way to do this. Do what feels right to you.

Some of my favorite angel crystals are selenite, angelite, and blue kyanite. They all have similar properties:

Selenite looks like a clear quartz crystal but is cloudy and softer. It comes in different sizes and shapes. I have a nice-sized piece carved in the form of a tower. It is fantastic for clearing your auric field as it helps you to attain mental clarity. While selenite can have a calming effect, it is also such a highly charged crystal that it can assist you in raising your vibrations to that higher frequency that enables one to make angelic contact.

Selenite never needs cleansing or recharging. If you have other crystals that need cleansing, you can place them in a pouch or box with a piece of selenite to help keep them clear. As powerful a crystal as selenite is, it is very fragile and should be handled with care. Water can damage selenite, so don't get it wet.

Angelite is commonly a sky-blue stone with flecks of white and brown. These flecks give the appearance of different images on the stone. I have one that looks like it has little angels, birds, and animals on it. Angelite is formed from celestite (another angel crystal) that has been compressed over millions of years.

Angelite can assist you in elevating your consciousness during meditation to frequencies that allow for telepathic communication. It is also another very peaceful and calming stone that encourages compassion.

Blue kyanite is a bright blue stone with flecks of white. It is my absolute favorite angel crystal. When highly polished for jewelry, it makes a lovely piece. One of my favorite rings is a large blue kyanite stone set in sterling silver.

Blue kyanite is naturally attuned to the angelic realms. It is also a stone that never requires cleansing. It is an excellent stone to work with for balancing your chakras. It heightens clairaudience. It wasn't long after I began wearing and working with blue kyanite that I began hearing my angels.

Angel Numbers

Amongst the many ways angels deliver messages to us are what have come to be known as *angel numbers*. Angel numbers are usually reoccurring patterns of repeating numbers; for example, 11:11, 111, 222, 333, 444, and so on. They may also come as a random sequence of numbers you repeatedly see, like 414 or 2034. The numbers can be in any combination, and there isn't any particular combination that holds more importance or relevance than another; it's the fact that you keep seeing that same combination wherever you go. That's significant because it's a prompt that your angels are trying to tell you something.

The concept of angel numbers is like that of numerology. Numerology is the study of vibrational patterns of numbers from 1 through 9. Each number's vibrational energy has a unique pattern, and numbers run in predictable cycles. This concept is based on theories from the great Greek philosopher Pythagoras.

The following is a list of some of the basic meanings of the numbers 0 through 9 as they pertain to angel number messages:

0 - Symbolizes God. It represents our connection to Source and our unlimited potential when we "Let go and let God." Number sequences containing 0 let us know that God is speaking to us.

1 - Pay attention to what you think because your thoughts manifest into reality. New opportunities are presented.

2 - Keep the faith! Trust in God and the angels. Remember to ask and believe so that you are open to receiving Divine wisdom and blessings.

3 - The ascended masters, like Jesus, Mother Mary, St. Therese, Buddha, Kuan Yin, Moses, etc., are supporting you now. You are co-creating with the support of one or more of them.

4 - The angels are supporting you now.

5 - Go with the flow of the shifts that are taking place now. This number can also indicate that it is time for a change if you've been considering it.

6 - Balance is essential, especially where material matters are concerned. Release your worries regarding your finances to the angels. Harmony in relationships can be realized with the support and guidance of your angels.

7 - You are becoming more aware of Divine guidance, and more opportunities will be presented to you. You are advancing in your spiritual growth and development.

8 - Abundance can be yours. Keep honing your skills. What you put your loving energy into brings you great rewards. Good Karma!

9 - You are ready to achieve your life's purpose. Your life's purpose includes spiritual work. You are near the completion of a significant life cycle. You are ready to advance to the next level in your spirituality.

Repeating numbers further enhances the qualities of each number. So, for example, if you notice the number "111" showing up a lot, it's the angels' way of letting you know that your thoughts are highly charged right now and manifesting rapidly, so pay attention to what you are thinking about because that's what you are attracting into your life. The number "11" is a similar message; however, "111" is more powerful and urgent.

Let's look at number "414." The number "1" is surrounded by "4" on both sides. Look at the list above and combine the meanings. "The angels are supporting you now. Pay attention to what you think because your thoughts manifest into reality. New opportunities are presented." The second number, "4," encourages you to trust that the angels fully support you, so you should stay focused on what you want to achieve because they act as your safety net.

Angel numbers are one of the many ways our angels will send us signs and communicate messages. They use things in our everyday lives and environment to get our attention and a point across to us. So, the next time you take notice of specific reoccurring numbers when you glance at the clock on the wall, the license plate on the car in front of you, or the number on your hotel room door, know that this may not be just a coincidence, it can be an important and meaningful message from your angels.

The Numerology of Archangel Names

The concept of angel numbers and numerology is also rooted in the art of gematria. Gematria is the art of finding numeric values and is used in analyzing both biblical names and the names of angels. According to Kabalarian philosophy, each letter of the Hebrew alphabet has a numeric value, and the calculated numeric values in a word reveal an archetypical fundamental nature.

It is intriguing to take note of the numerological patterns that occur in angel names. When analyzed through Pythagorean numerology (where each letter of the alphabet is associated with a single digit number from 1 through 9), all angel names contain either or any combination of the numbers 3, 6, or 9, which represent creativity and communication "3," nurturing and harmony "6," and philanthropy and accomplishment "9."

When examining the numerology of angel name numbers for the soul urge, destiny, and personality numbers, you will always find a 3, 6, or 9 in your numerology calculations for angel names. You can find free Pythagorean numerology calculators on the Internet.

<u>Let's take a look at the numerology of Archangel Michael's name</u>:

Michael – Soul Urge: 6, Destiny: 6, Personality: 9

The letters in the name "Michael" contain the numerological vibrations of "6" twice and a "9." Since the quality of "6" is doubled, it can be seen as the master number, "66," indicating that Archangel Michael has the power to expand consciousness and provide encouragement to seek a larger purpose in life. Master number "66" indicates that Archangel Michael is a powerful archangel. In contrast, he holds the numerological vibration of the "Master Lover/ Artisan." He can thus empower one to achieve self-confidence and satisfaction in work that leads to the achievement of one's life purpose.

<u>Here's an example of the numerology of Archangel Gabriel's name</u>:

Gabriel – Soul Urge: 6, Destiny: 9, and Personality: 3

The letters in the name "Gabriel" contain the numerological vibrations of all three numbers found in all angel names, suggesting that Archangel Gabriel is a powerful archangel. His name implies the soul urge for nurturing and harmony "6", the destiny of philanthropy and accomplishment "9", and the personality of the creator and communicator "3."

You can see where I'm going with this concept now. The study of numerology as it pertains to angel number messages and angel names is a fascinating topic!

Exercise #5

Choose a method for which to do a reading for someone. This can be done using cards, angel numbers, angel crystals, or intuitively without any tools, it's up to you. Allow the person you are reading for to choose whether they would like to ask a specific question or receive a general angel message.

Follow the procedures for preparing yourself for a reading – say your prayer of protection, clear any tools that you plan to use for the reading, call upon the angels and any spirit guides you may work with and ask to see, hear, feel, or know whatever is most important and in the highest good of all concerned in the matter of the reading...

Share the messages that you receive and pay close attention to the response of the person you are reading for so that you can later note in your journal, any feedback you received on the reading along with whatever you can recall of the reading.

Your Notes:

Working As An Angel Practitioner

Working as an angel practitioner can be very rewarding in numerous ways. Aside from being a business that you can conduct from almost anywhere, anytime, the benefits are many. When you work as an angel practitioner, you are charging up your own spiritual batteries as well as that of others. Plus, you receive good karma and blessings for sharing the love and light of the Divine.

When you work with the angelic realm, it's like a natural boost to your own vibrational energy. Once you are open to receiving the love, light, and guidance of the angels, you will feel safe, calm, confident, and happy. You know that you are never alone and will always be guided toward that which is in your highest good. You will be able to do what your soul incarnated into this lifetime to do.

You will find that the more you work with the angels, the more you will make connections with better people. Even though you may still come across people who can be draining, you will be better equipped to deal with them. The more experienced an angel practitioner you become, the less difficult and needy people will be able to drain you. You will know how to protect yourself and set healthy boundaries.

The more you work with the angels, the more you will notice that you are inspired and motivated. You will have the enthusiasm to start the projects you may have been putting off AND you will have the drive to complete them! You will be amazed at what you can accomplish when you work with the angels. It is truly a blessing to do this type of work. It doesn't feel like work at all.

There might still be days when your vibrational energy is lower and you will need a boost, but the good news is that you will be able to raise it again with the help of your angels. Life is a series of ups and downs. Things can still go wrong, but when you know that you have angelic support and guidance available to you, you will be able to get past any difficulties that life may throw your way and rise above it, coming out better and stronger than you were before.

Working as an angel practitioner, you can choose the time and place where you will work. You will have very flexible hours. You can work from your home or another location. You can do readings, you can teach classes and/or facilitate workshops, you can write about angels, you can draw or paint angels, you can run motivational groups or support groups, the opportunities are only limited to your imagination and free will.

When you choose to follow this spiritual path, it becomes a path of lifelong learning. You don't just take a course, or read a book, and stop there. You continue to build your knowledge and hone your skills by reading more books, taking more coursework, attending meetings and lectures, joining group discussions, and so forth. We live in a changing world and evolving universe, so we need to keep abreast of these changes and learn how to best evolve spiritually within it.

Building Confidence as an Angel Practitioner

As an angel practitioner, it is important to have confidence in your abilities to communicate with the angels and deliver messages to your clients. Here are some tips and techniques, as well as a prayer, a specific archangel to call upon, and an affirmation, to help you build and strengthen your confidence as you work with the angels:

First, let's start with the foundation of confidence: believing in yourself. It is essential to believe in your ability to connect with the angels and deliver accurate messages. This belief will allow you to approach each session with a positive mindset, which will in turn help you to feel more confident in your abilities.

Next, it is important to trust in the guidance of the angels. The angels are here to help and support us, and they will always provide us with loving and accurate messages. By trusting in their guidance, you can have confidence in the messages that you are delivering to your clients.

To help build your trust in the angels, you can call upon the archangel Michael for protection and guidance. Michael is the angel of strength and courage and can help you to feel more confident and assured as you work with the angels. You can say the following prayer to call upon Michael:

> *"Dear Archangel Michael, please surround me with your protective and loving energy as I work with the angels. Help me to trust in the*

> *guidance and messages that I receive, knowing that they are for my highest good and the highest good of my clients. Thank you for your strength and support."*

It is also helpful to practice, practice, practice! The more you work with the angels, the more comfortable and confident you will become in your abilities. Don't be afraid to ask for help or guidance from other angel practitioners or teachers, as they can provide valuable support and feedback as you develop your skills.

Another way to build confidence is to stay open and receptive to learning and growth. This can include reading books, attending workshops or seminars, and simply being open to learning and expanding your understanding. The more knowledge and understanding you have about working with the angels, the more confidence you will feel in your abilities.

Here is an affirmation that you can use to boost your confidence as an angel practitioner:

> *"I am a confident and skilled angel practitioner, connected to the love and guidance of the angels. I trust in my abilities and the messages that I receive, and I am open to learning and growth. I am worthy and deserving of confidence, and I embrace my unique gifts and skills as I work with the angels."*

You can repeat this affirmation to yourself anytime you need a confidence boost or reminder of your skills and abilities as an angel practitioner. It can also be helpful to write the affirmation down and keep it with you as a reminder of your strength and confidence.

Finally, remember to take care of yourself and prioritize self-care. When we are stressed or overwhelmed, it can be difficult to feel confident in anything. By taking care of your physical, emotional, and spiritual well-being, you can maintain a clear and grounded energy which will help you feel more confident.

Bringing it All Together

Now that you've had the chance to read about and explore some foundational tools and techniques for working with the angels, practice with each. Take note of the modalities that interest you and complement your learning, working, and communicating style.

For those who may have already been working with the angels before reading this book, perhaps some of the information in this guide has led you to discover a new modality for connecting with the angels you hadn't considered before. Either way, I hope you have come away with the desire to continue to work with the angels and explore other methods for connecting with Spirit and the angelic realm for Divine wisdom and guidance.

Angel Messages

What the Angels Told Me...

As an angel practitioner, I make the time to meditate and connect with my angels as means of quieting my thinking mind while fortifying my intuitive abilities. During these periods of meditation, I often channel meaningful wisdom from the angelic realm.

I have edited the information below so that the grammar is clear and concise. When these insights come to me, there are some succinct words, but most of it comes in the form of a sense of "knowing." The following is a sampling of some of the mystical insights that the angels have shared with me:

- Our guardian angel is the same guardian angel throughout all of our lifetimes.
- When we are grateful for the littlest things, we receive the biggest boosts to our vibrational energy.
- Archangels are activated by God when we call upon them. In a way, God recreates them each time someone calls upon them. The names we use to call

upon them with invoke the specific blessings that they can bestow upon us.

- So, for example, when you think or say, Archangel Raphael's name, you are thinking or saying, "God heals."

- Your level of faith in Archangel Raphael's ability to heal increases or decreases the strength in that healing power.

- Being that God releases that part of Himself to you in the form of an angelic blessing (if it is part of His Divine will and for your highest good), this is how this power is available simultaneously to whoever requests it.

- God did not create humans in His own image; rather, He created our souls in His own image.

- Your thoughts are a language. Thoughts ARE the language of telepathy. Telepathy IS the Universal language of the spiritual realms and it's what allows us to be able to communicate with angels, spirit guides, departed loved ones, and other discarnate entities.

- Archangels Metatron and Sandalphon can both help to speed up the answers to our prayers. They are especially good at this because both of these archangels were the only angels to actually have ever lived human lifetimes on Earth and thus, can relate to our sense of time and space.

- Your negative thinking is to angels like a snowstorm is to your mail carrier... Your mail will be delivered, but it might be delayed.

- When you focus on the solution instead of the problem, you make it easier for the angels to assist you and accelerate the arrival of blessings that God has in store for you.

- When many stand in faith, something magical happens!

- Your intention will manifest as it is your soul's true desire. Your intention is your free will in action. Your intentions create your reality. So be mindful of your true intentions – the will of your soul, as it will come to be.

- Intuition is more important than psychic ability. Our angels speak to us through intuition. Intuition is in the present. Psychic sense can stretch from the past throughout the future. The past cannot be changed. The future is volatile. The present is happening now and is the most important because it essentially creates our future. The present is where we have the most control.

- Spirit is an unseen energy that helps to connect us with all that is...

Resources For Angel Practitioners & Enthusiasts

Maria's Website: https://www.MariaGMaas.com

- **Angel Oracle Cards Deck:** *The Angelic View Oracle Cards with Guidebook & Journal*
- Book a Reading with Maria
- Read Maria's Blog
- Subscribe to Maria's Newsletter
- **Radio Shows & Podcasts:** *The Angelic View Show* and *Angelic Realms Radio*
- **Courses:** *Certified Angel Practitioner™ (CAP™)*
- *Mastering the Art of Angel, Oracle, & Tarot Card Reading™*

Social Media:

- Like the *IAAP* on Facebook at https://facebook.com/angelpractitioners
- Like Maria G. Maas on Facebook at https://facebook.com/mariasmysticinsights

- Follow Maria G. Maas on Twitter at https://twitter.com/mysticinsights
- Join the *IAAP Members* private Facebook group at https://www.facebook.com/groups/iaapmembers
- Join *Tarot, Angels, & Spirituality* private Facebook group at https://www.facebook.com/groups/TarotandSpirituality

Professional Organization:

International Association of Angel Practitioners (IAAP)
https://www.AngelPractitioners.com

- Silver Membership – Free
- Gold Membership – Fee-based
- Angel Courses (with option to become certified via the IAAP)
- Directory of Angel Practitioners

Photo Album

Over the years, I've been blessed to have the opportunity to study under some highly skilled and world-renowned authors and teachers. I thought I'd share a few photos from my personal collection with you.

Mary K. Greer and Maria G. Maas – July 2021

Mary K. Greer and Maria G. Maas – June 2010

Colette Baron-Reid and Maria G. Maas - July 2011

Maria G. Maas and Lisa Williams - August 2013

Author's Note

I hope you enjoyed this book. If you have not yet enrolled in the *Certified Angel Practitioner™ Course* and would like to sign up or learn more about it, please visit www.MariaGMaas.com or www.AngelPractitioners.com for more information.

Wishing you love, light, and angel blessings...

~ Maria G. Maas, Angel-Intuitive Medium & Spiritual Teacher
President & Cofounder of www.AngelPractitioners.com and the *International Association of Angel Practitioners (IAAP)*
Founder of www.MariaGMaas.com

ABOUT THE AUTHOR

Maria G. Maas is an angel-intuitive medium and creator of the *Certified Angel Practitioner™ Course*. She is president and cofounder of <u>AngelPractitioners.com</u> and the *International Association of Angel Practitioners (IAAP)*.

Maria also hosts <u>*The Angelic View Radio Show*</u> and has broadcasted hundreds of episodes of talk-radio shows since 2012. On *The Angelic View,* listeners are educated about angels, tarot, spirituality, and more. It is a live call-in show where Maria also provides complimentary readings and angel messages for callers.

Maria G. Maas became a serious student of spiritual pathways and tools in the mid-1990s and has earned the following credentials: Certified Tarot Master, Certified Angel Card Reader, and Certified Master Angel Practitioner. Maria is a professional educator and holds a master's degree from Long Island University, CW Post.

Maria, her husband, Arthur, and their two adorable, pampered cats enjoy living the snowbird lifestyle and having homes in New York's Hudson Valley and Southwest Florida's Gulf Coast.

Printed in the United States
by Baker & Taylor Publisher Services